HEY, GIFTED GIRL

Education Edition

By Dr. Kimberly R. Mack

Copyright 2022 by Dr. Kimberly R. Mack

Kimberly Mack LLC
@purposedrivened
Fairfield Township, OH 45011

All rights reserved. No part of this book may be reproduced, transmitted, or stored in any information retrieval system in any form or by any means, electronic, mechanical, photocopying, recording, or otherwise without written permission of the publisher

Printed in the USA by Kindle Direct Publishing

Education Edition

ISBN: 978-1-7378960-6-7

Orvetta Mack
1935-2019

Dedicated to my mom, who encouraged me and affirmed my giftedness

Rev. Will Mack
1926-2012

Dedicated to my dad, who challenged me to prove my giftedness

When I look in the mirror
What do I see?
I see a gifted girl
Looking back at me.

She is kind. She is patient
and as pretty as can be.
I smile at that gifted girl
Looking back at me.

When she walks in a room
Her head is held high,
Because she knows in her heart
Everything will be alright.

As she walks into school
she is ready to learn.
She knows she has the answer
when the teacher calls her turn.

When I look in the mirror
What do I see?
I see a beautiful girl
Looking back at me.

She is kind. She is patient
and as pretty as can be.
I smile at that beautiful girl
Looking back at me.

When she gets home from school
She already knows the rules.
Her bookbag she unpacks
then, goes to get a snack.

Once her snack is finished
to do homework she quickly goes.
After that, there's time to play
Before her parents return home.

When I look in the mirror
What do I see?
I see a dancing girl
Looking back at me.

She is kind. She is patient
and as pretty as can be.
I smile at that dancing girl
Looking back at me.

No matter what she faces,
She stands up very tall.
Won't let problems get her down.
On road blocks she won't fall.

the problems may be much.
they even challenge greatness.
She knows like the gifted do.
they are just a test of fitness.

When I look in the mirror
What do I see?
I see a friendly girl
Looking back at me.

She is kind. She is patient
and as pretty as can be.
I smile at that friendly girl
Looking back at me.

When you look in the mirror
What do you see?
You are a gifted, talented girl
just as you should be.

You are gifted.
You are beautiful.
You are dancing.
You are friendly.
You are kind.
You are patient
and as pretty as can be.
Just smile, smile,
and smile some more
at that gifted girl you see.

Other Children's Books
By Dr. Kimberly Mack

My Gift
Children need to know that they have gifts and talents to share with the world. In My Gift, Isaiah spends the day with his Dad and realizes he has a special gift. It's helping hands!

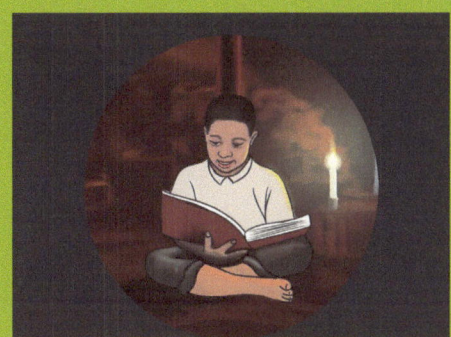

Courage to Achieve Great Things: The Life of John P. Parker
Sharing the stories of African-Americans who achieved extraordinary prominence, this book tells the story of a great hero with the Underground Railroad.

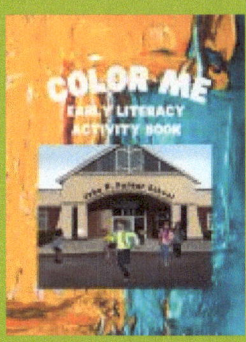

Color Me: Early Literacy Activity Book
This activity book helps early learners to practice skills while learning about Global Environmental Literacy.

www.ingramcontent.com/pod-product-compliance
Lightning Source LLC
Chambersburg PA
CBHW061400090426
42743CB00002B/82